William Wallace: The Life and Legacy

By Charles River Editors

A statute commemorating Wallace at the Scottish National Portrait Gallery in Edinburgh.

About Charles River Editors

Charles River Editors provides superior editing and original writing services across the digital publishing industry, with the expertise to create digital content for publishers across a vast range of subject matter. In addition to providing original digital content for third party publishers, we also republish civilization's greatest literary works, bringing them to new generations of readers via ebooks.

Introduction

Early 20th century depiction of Wallace in H E Marshall's *Scotland's Story*.

William Wallace (?-1305)

"A false usurper sinks in every foe

And liberty returns with every blow." – Blind Harry

William Wallace is one of the most famous freedom fighters in history, and over 700 years after his death he is still remembered as Scotland's beloved hero. But while the movie

Braveheart helped make him a household name, and he is commemorated across Scotland as a natural leader and a loyal son of his homeland, he is also "the most mysterious of the leaders of the Scottish resistance to Edward I."[1] This is because, paradoxically, the very famous soldier is also one of the least well known. In fact, the mystery surrounding Wallace is figuring out precisely, or even vaguely, who he was. Where did this champion of Scottish independence come from? Who was his family? What did he do before emerging from obscurity with the brutal murder of William Heselrig, the English sheriff of Lanark, in May 1297? So little evidence on Wallace's life exists that answering even the most basic questions about him can be a challenge.

That said, as one scholar perceptively notes, "the facts are not the reason why he is remembered as a meaningful historical actor." [2] For the admirers Wallace has accumulated over the centuries, the idealized version of what he stood for - weak over strong, justice over injustice, the will of the people over the might of the powerful - is infinitely more important than the historical man himself. Similarly, his English detractors have also focused on image over substance through the years, depicting Wallace as a heartless brute, a cruel traitor, and a blood-hungry outlaw. Whether he's depicted as an icon of Scottish resistance or a symbol of disloyalty and treachery, William Wallace is as much an idea as he was an actual figure of the Scottish Wars of Independence.

How does one study someone about whom so little is actually known and whose idealized (or vilified) image has overshadowed his actions? Piecing together the story of William Wallace's life is an exercise in asking more questions than can be answered, and often in looking at just as much conjecture as proof. While acknowledging that many aspects of his life will remain obscure, *William Wallace: The Life and Legacy of the Scottish Freedom Fighter* attempts to separate fact from fiction while looking at the life and fighting of the man who inspired *Braveheart*. Along with pictures and a bibliography, you will learn about William Wallace like you never have before, in no time at all.

---

[1] Michael Prestwich, "Review of *William Wallace* by Andrew Fisher," *The American Historical Review*, Vol. 93, No. 5 (Dec., 1988), p. 1312.
[2] G. Morton. *William Wallace: Man and Myth* (Stroud, 2001).

Chapter 1: Blind Harry and the Wallace Legend

It is impossible to discuss William Wallace without making reference to Blind Harry, or Henry the Minstrel (c.1440-c.1492), the 15th century bard credited with writing the earliest surviving account of Wallace's life: the epic poem "The History of the Life and Heroic Actions of the Renowned Sir William Wallace, General and Governor of Scotland." Written somewhere around 1474-1479, roughly 170 years after the warrior's death, the epic contains more than 11,000 lines on Wallace's exploits and is peppered with a great deal of embellishment and fiction. But despite the fact it is heavily scrutinized over its accuracy (or lack thereof), Blind Harry's epic has framed the way the Scottish warrior is remembered and has shaped what many think of as the "historical" Wallace.

15th century financial accounts show that Blind Harry earned a living reciting poetry and song and had performed in the court of King James IV, as well as other noble venues. Thus, not surprisingly, the Wallace he depicts is a blend of folklore and literary conventions deliberately intended to portray the warrior as a "gracious god of Scotland," rather than some ordinary Scotsman from a middling-rank noble family.[3] It is also important to note that Harry performed mainly for anti-English audiences who were hungry for tales of rebellion and misdeeds against their southern neighbor. Moreover, many nobles found in Harry's work the opportunity to attack the reigning Scottish monarch, King James III, who was perceived as supporting pro-English policies far too much. Having Harry recite his heavily anti-English biography of Wallace was likely a way for many Scottish nobles of the 1470s to promote indirect criticism of James III.

---

[3] John Balaban, "Blind Harry and 'The Wallace'" *The Chaucer Review*, Vol. 8, No. 3 (Winter, 1974), p. 250.

Portrait of James III, King of Scots

Whatever their motives, Scottish nobles taking in Harry's epic would have heard of a robust and indefatigable Wallace, a Scottish hero who wanted nothing other than to destroy the hated English. He was a larger-than-life champion who made the ultimate sacrifice for his people: "Thus, we have a heroic figure in size and deed, who gave his life to his country – Right sooth it is, a martyr Wallace was." With lines like that, it's easy to understand how Harry's Wallace would appeal to the Scots and the anti-English sentiments that prevailed in the 1470s, but what might have surprised even Harry himself is the lasting appeal his work on Wallace would come to have on the Scots for centuries after his death. Since the 1470s, Blind Harry's biography has constituted the popular version of Wallace's life and was even the template for the 1995 film

Braveheart. It also helped that an adaptation of the poem was completed by William Hamilton and published in 1722, making Harry's work more accessible to a broader audience.[4] Indeed, it was this later version that fueled the imagination of many writers and poets, including the 18th century Scottish poet Robert Burns, whose 1793 patriotic song "Scots Wha Hae," or "Scots, who have," begins with the line "Scots, who have with Wallace bled."

Despite its enduring popularity, Harry's epic retelling of Wallace's deeds is barely recognizable when it comes to history, as it is undoubtedly more fiction than fact. Nevertheless, by virtue of its long-standing prevalence, the Wallace it depicts is the Wallace of the popular imagination. Thus, to arrive at a more authentic view of the "real" Scottish leader, historians must first dismantle the legend.

Chapter 2: Wallace's Early Years

The process of distinguishing fact from fiction in Wallace's life begins with the Scot's origins and family. It was long thought, based on Blind Harry's account, that Wallace's father was a certain Malcolm who came from the area of Renfrew, west of Glasgow. The genealogies constructed around this claim declare Wallace to be the great-great-grandson of Richard Wallace, a vassal to Walter Fitzalan. In 1136, Fitzalan entered the service of David I, king of Scotland, as a steward of the household, and Richard Wallace is presumed to have been part of a flood of English-born men who followed Fitzalan (also English) north to serve the Scottish monarchy. Though the exact date of Richard's move to Scotland is unknown, most believe it took place during the reign of Walter I, which began in 1166.

It is believed that Wallace's father Malcolm had at least five children, including William, his two brothers John and Malcolm (at least one of whom was older than William), and possibly two sisters as well. As a younger son, Wallace could not inherit the family estate and thus would have had to seek a living beyond his kin. One of Blind Harry's best-known claims was that Wallace had planned for a life in the Church, a common vocational choice for younger sons. Tutored by a maternal uncle who was a priest, Wallace, Blind Harry boasted, was extremely well educated, knew both Latin and Greek, and possessed a particularly profound knowledge of the Bible. In this telling, William's progress toward the contemplative life would have proceeded uninterruptedly if only Edward I of England had not set out to bring Scotland under his domination. Enraged by the monarch's actions, Wallace abandoned his plans of joining the Church and began his famous fight against the English, a fight that made him one of Scotland's most celebrated figures.

---

[4] James E. Fraser, "'A Sawn from a Raven': William Wallace, Brucean Propaganda, and "Gesta Annalia" II," *The Scottish Historical Review*, Vol. 81, No. 211, (April, 2002), p. 1.

Portrait of Edward I of England

Blind Harry's version of Wallace's early years is unquestionably an absorbing narrative, especially the future leader's dramatic shift from tranquil preparation for life in the church to the tooth-and-nail existence of a warrior, and over the centuries, this extraordinary story has been the definitive account of the hero's early life. It was believed to be wholly credible largely because Harry himself had claimed to have based his account of Wallace on a Latin prose description of the warrior's life written by one of his contemporaries, John Blair. A Benedictine monk, Blair is understood to have been Wallace's personal chaplain, and he later wrote extensively about his famous patron. Though his work has long been lost, Blind Harry's presumed access to the writings of one of Wallace's contemporaries lent great legitimacy to his own work, since it was assumed the bard was drawing from an informed and authentic source.[5]

However, since so much of Wallace's life as told by Blind Harry has turned out to be more myth than fact, most scholars now dismiss every aspect of Harry's poem, which leaves almost nothing known for sure about Wallace's origins, family, and early years. As historian Andrew Fisher put it, William Wallace is "at best a shadowy figure and likely to remain so."[6] Besides a rough estimate of his birth year, which most believe to be around 1270, specific details, such as place of birth, exact date of birth, or the location and condition of the Wallace family, remain elusive.

Why have historians cast aside Blind Harry's account of Wallace's family? The discovery of new and, according to Fisher, "indisputable" evidence shows that Wallace was not the son of Sir Malcolm Wallace of Elderslie in Renfrew but of a certain Alan Wallace. On becoming Guardian of Scotland following the battle of Stirling Bridge in 1297, Wallace sent letters to the public officials of the German towns of Lübeck and Hamburg for the purpose of recommencing trade with the Hanseatic League, and one of these missives, known as the Lübeck letter, has survived.[7] It is one of the few surviving artifacts that can be connected to Wallace, and most importantly, Wallace used a seal on the letter containing the following inscription: "[Wilelm]vs Filius Alani Walais" (William, son of Alan Wallace). The inscription was a clear indication of the father's name.[8]

This revelation about Wallace's true parentage undermined centuries of studies about his family line (long linked to Malcolm and considered to be in the west of Scotland) and raises new possibilities about the Scottish hero's origins and early years. Of course, identifying precisely who Alan was has been historians' primary concern. The Ragman Roll of 1296, a collection of documents containing the names of the Scottish nobility and gentry who subscribed allegiance to King Edward I of England, provides a tantalizing clue. It lists an Alan Wallace as a landholder in Ayrshire, in southwest Scotland. If this Alan is indeed Wallace's father, then this raises numerous new questions about the Wallace clan and allows for a different picture of how Wallace spent his early years.

The most pressing question this piece of evidence raises has to do with the family's political loyalties. It has long been assumed that the Wallace clan was united in its anti-English sentiment and in its support of rebellion against Edward I, but if the Alan Wallace listed in the Ragman Roll was indeed Wallace's father, this evidence forces scholars to reconsider this notion. As hard as it may be to believe, the Ragman Roll begs the question of whether Wallace's own father supported Edward I. Otherwise, why would he pledge allegiance to Edward I by signing his name to this document?

---

[5] For a more extensive discussion of Blind Harry's work, see Graham McLennan, ed., *The Wild Flower: Blind Harry's Life of Wallace the Outlaw* (Caberra, 1993).

[6] Andrew Fisher, *William Wallace* (Edinburgh: John Donald Publishers, 1986).

[7] This letter is kept in the National Archives of Lübeck.

[8] Metal casts of the front and back of the seal were made in 1911. In 1999, they were discovered tucked away in a small box in Glasgow's Mitchell Library.

It's altogether possible that the appearance of Alan Wallace's name on the Ragman Roll should not be taken to mean that he was opposed to the Scottish rebellion against Edward I. Like many Scots at this time, Alan was probably acting as a realist, toeing the line in order to protect his property and to survive in the challenging and quickly changing political context. What's more, signing the Ragman Roll was not necessarily a voluntary act, as many people were forced to put their names on it regardless of their actual political stance. It's possible the Wallace clan was united in its opposition to the English, and at the same time, the Alan listen in the Ragman Roll may not be the father of the famed William Wallace anyway.

The clues left by the seal Wallace used on the Lübeck letters are not related exclusively to his father, because the images it contains also reveal something about what the young Scotsman might have done before his meteoric rise to become Guardian of Scotland in 1297. While the front of the seal displays a Scottish Lion rampant (the Royal Arms of Scotland), the reverse shows a particularly telling image of a strung bow with an arrow. This does not appear to be part of a coat of arms, as the bow and arrow are not displayed on a shield, the usual device to convey heraldic imagery. Rather, the seal merely shows a hand drawing an arrow on a bow. Though Wallace's seal is small and the imagery on it is faint, it nonetheless casts strong doubt on Blind Harry's claim that prior to the Scottish Wars of Independence, Wallace was set to become a clergyman. It seems quite incongruous that someone bent on joining the Church would have a bow and arrow - symbols of warfare - as his seal, but as for the Wallace that the world is familiar with - the victor at Stirling Bridge, the brazen rebel against the English - the bow and arrow make perfect sense. It was also in line with the physical descriptions of Wallace spread during the 15th century. While it's highly unlikely Wallace was 7 feet tall as suggested by Harry, an abbot named Walter Bower described him at least a bit more realistically as "a tall man with the body of a giant ... with lengthy flanks ...broad in the hips, with strong arms and legs ... with all his limbs very strong and firm". This would certainly be in line with a professional soldier, and had the young Wallace earned his living through the bow and quiver, as the seal strongly indicates, it follows that one day he would emerge a great warrior, the colossal figure who routed the mighty English army in 1297.

What did it mean to earn one's living through the bow and quiver? One possibility is that Wallace was an outlaw, a suggestion many of his detractors made over the years. Another, and more plausible, likelihood is that the young Wallace made his way as a mercenary soldier, a profession many a younger son pursued and one that would help explain where he acquired the great military genius he showed in 1297 and 1298. In the late 13th century, there would have been several occasions for Wallace to find work as a soldier; at the time, Edward I was engaged in campaigns in France and in his successful effort to conquer Wales and incorporate it into the Kingdom of England. Either place would have provided Wallace the opportunity to hone his military skill. If he indeed did earn a living in the military, this would add an ironic twist to his life story, because it would likely mean the man who eventually crushed the English in 1297 acquired his military prowess from the very army he vanquished.[9]

While the notion of Wallace as a soldier fits well into his life narrative, it is, as are nearly all ideas about his early years, mere conjecture. Despite the new research possibilities the seal on the Lübeck letter opens, Wallace's origins and youth remain obscure, and efforts to reconstruct his lineage and early life are still just educated guessing games, bringing together and conjecturing about a handful of extant documents. What little is truly known about him relates primarily to the eight years between the Battle of Stirling Bridge in 1297 and his death in 1305. In this short window of time, William Wallace made himself known to posterity.

Chapter 3: 13th Century Scotland

While little is known about Wallace's background, there is solid knowledge of the era in which he grew up. The Scottish warrior was born during a period of relative peace in the Kingdom of Scotland, when relations with England were calm and cordial, and tensions with Norway, which had long been the kingdom's greatest cause of concern, had also settled. Responsible for this tranquility was the strong and charismatic monarch of Scotland, King Alexander III.

---

[9] For a discussion of the possibility that Wallace was a mercenary soldier in his youth, see Andrew Fisher, *William Wallace*, pp. 40-41.

A medieval depiction of Alexander III's coronation.

Alexander III ruled Scotland from 1249 until his death in 1286, and like his father, Alexander II (1214-1249), he had maintained fairly good relations with England and focused most of his efforts on the more tenuous affairs with Norway. Following the Battle of Largs in 1263 and the death of the King of Norway shortly thereafter, Alexander claimed the Isle of Man and the Western Isles (the Outer Hebrides) for Scotland. He later sealed the steady relations with Norway by arranging the marriage of his daughter Margaret to the Norse king Eric II.[10]

Alexander himself was married to another Margaret, the daughter of King Henry III of England and Eleanor of Provence, but the deaths of their three children in rapid succession in the 1280s (David, the youngest, died in 1281; Margaret in 1283; and Alexander, the heir apparent, in 1284) led to the crisis of succession that is considered one of the catalysts of the Scottish Wars of Independence. In 1284, he persuaded the "Estates" (Scotland's parliamentary body) to recognize his granddaughter Margaret, the "Maid of Norway," as his heir presumptive. Furthermore, by marrying for the second time in 1285 to Yolande de Deux, Alexander also apparently sought to produce a male heir.

However, all hopes for a stable succession were dashed when Alexander died suddenly in 1286 as a result of falling from his horse. His new wife was pregnant at the time, but she later lost the child[11], ensuring that Alexander's four-year-old granddaughter Margaret became the new Queen of Scotland. Perhaps not surprisingly, within just a few weeks, John Balliol, one of the main characters of the Scottish Wars of Independence, laid claim to the crown and was aided by John Comyn ("Red Comyn"), a Scottish nobleman who also figured prominently in the Wars. Their rebellion against Queen Margaret was subdued by Bruce family, but this clan's most famous member, Robert the Bruce, would also soon lay his own claim to the throne. In the case of Bruce, however, this did not happen until after the premature death of Queen Margaret in 1290, which occurred during her first journey to Scotland from her native Norway. Now with no obvious heir, Scotland stood on the precipice of internal warfare, with both John Balliol and Robert the Bruce angling aggressively for the crown.

---

[10] On the life and reign of Alexander III, see Marion Campbell, *Alexander III King of Scots* (House of Lochar, 1999).

[11] It is not clear whether Yolande suffered a miscarriage or whether the baby was stillborn.

Medieval depiction of John Balliol and his wife.

A statue of Robert the Bruce at Edinburgh Castle

To avoid civil war, the Scots, led by the Guardians of Scotland (the de facto heads of state during the Queen's minority), turned to King Edward of England for help in the succession crisis, and he initiated a process known as the Great Cause to determine who had the most legitimate case to become Scotland's next monarch. Naturally, Edward I also exploited the situation to increase his own authority in the region by refusing to act as arbiter in Scotland's affairs unless his feudal lordship over the territory was recognized first. Edward left the Scots with little choice; when he met with the Guardians at Norham, just south of the Scottish border, in 1291, he had his army standing by to exert pressure on the Scots. This, along with the threat of many Scottish nobles losing their estates in England should the king's demands not be met, prompted the Guardians to give in. The English king was subsequently recognized as Lord Paramount of Scotland.[12]

His status as Scotland's overlord confirmed, Edward proceeded with the Great Cause, holding numerous meetings at Berwick in northern England between May and August 1291, with no less than 13 nobles coming forward to claim the throne. The focus, however, was on the two leading claimants: Balliol and Bruce. Balliol's claim to the crown was based on a connection to King David I (r. 1124-1153) on his maternal side. His grandmother was the eldest daughter of David,

---

[12] On Edward I and the Great Cause, see Michael Prestwich, "Edward I (1239-1307)," *Oxford Dictionary of National Biography* (Oxford: Oxford University Press, 2004).

Earl of Huntingdon, who was the son of Henry, Earl of Huntingdon, who was the son of King David I. Robert the Bruce was also a descendant of King David and came from the same line as Balliol on his maternal side, but Bruce's mother (who was also Balliol's grandmother) was the second daughter of David, Earl of Huntingdon, and thus slightly further from King David in terms of proximity of blood. As a result, on November 17, 1292, in the Great Hall of Berwick Castle, Edward chose John Balliol as Scotland's monarch and designated Balliol's son Edward as his heir. With the support of the majority of Scottish nobles, including John Comyn, who was married to Balliol's sister but who himself had also laid claim to the throne, Balliol was officially declared King of the Scots on November 30, 1292, St. Andrew's Day.

Some historians argue that Edward chose Balliol figuring he would be a weak king, and tellingly, as early as December 26, 1292, King John swore homage to Edward at Newcastle upon Tyne. Thereafter the English monarch wasted no time in exercising the authority he had coerced from the Scots. He treated the country as a feudal vassal state, demanding it acknowledge his legal authority over the Scottish monarch, that it help bear the costs for defending England, and that it give military support in the war against France. Balliol was humiliated and antagonized by members of Bruce's faction, and as Edward continued to make demands of Balliol, a deep anti-English sentiment took hold in Scotland.[13]

By 1295, a group of 12 Scottish nobles, consisting of four bishops, four earls and four barons, seized control of the situation from the weakened Balliol and maneuvered behind the scenes to negotiate a treaty with King Philip IV of France. An agreement, known later as the Auld Alliance, was signed in October 1295 and stipulated that if either country was attacked by England, the other would come to its defense. This move directly challenged all claims Edward had over Scotland, but the French king did not engage in this alliance for altruistic purposes. He shared Scotland's desire to curtail English expansion, but he also shared England's desire to exercise influence over Scotland. Furthermore, upon signing the Auld Alliance, it was decided that King Philip's niece would marry the heir to the Scottish throne, King John Balliol's son Edward. In the end, the marriage never took place, but the marriage agreement itself reveals the pragmatic political ploys typical of medieval Europe.

When Edward learned of the secret Franco-Scottish alliance, he began preparing his forces to attack Scotland while also fortifying his northern defenses and solidifying relations with various anti-Balliol Scots, most notably Robert the Bruce. Following the outcome of the Great Cause, the Bruce clan had refused to support John Balliol's kingship, but it also remained close with Edward. In retaliation for Bruce's resistance, King John seized the Bruce family estates in Carrick in southwest Scotland and gave them to John Comyn. Thus, it likely came as no surprise to King John that his directive to all able-bodied Scotsmen to bear arms and assemble at Caddonlee near the English border in March 1296 and prepare for war with England went

---

[13] On John Balliol, see G. P. Stell, "John [John de Balliol] (c.1248x50-1314)," *Oxford Dictionary of National Biography* (Oxford: Oxford University Press, 2004).

ignored by Robert the Bruce.

Within a year of John's directive, William Wallace would burst onto the military scene in Scotland. His actions in campaigns throughout 1297 struck fear in many an English army commander, and he sealed his own place in history by becoming one of the most formidable leaders of the Scottish uprising against Edward's rule.

Chapter 4: The Scottish Wars of Independence

The Wars of Scottish Independence are generally divided into two wars. The First War lasted from 1296-1328, while the Second War lasted from 1332-1357. Wallace figured prominently in the first decade of the First War, from his initial campaigns in 1297 (most notably the Battle of Stirling Bridge) until his death in 1305. When he rose up against Edward in 1297, he brought a new fervor and passion to the Scottish rebellion, but in order to fully comprehend the extent to which Wallace was a pivotal figure in the war, it is necessary to understand the humiliation and ignominy the Scots suffered in 1296.

The First War began with Edward's bold and brutal sacking of Berwick in March 1296. The city, which sits on the border with England, was viciously attacked, and as many as 10,000 inhabitants were killed. Though the garrison attempted to defend the castle, they were eventually overtaken and forced to surrender[14], and with that, Edward remained in Berwick for a month in the hopes of achieving a swift conquest of Scotland if not a full capitulation. However, on April 5, Edward received a communication from King John renouncing his fealty to the English monarch. The Scots were not yielding.

Edward subsequently focused on the next objective in his campaign: the castle at Dunbar, only a few miles up the coast from Berwick. The castle belonged to the Earl of March, who had sided with Edward, but his wife had remained a fierce patriot and allowed her fellow Scots to occupy the stronghold. Edward sent John Balliol's own father-in-law, John de Warenne, 6th Earl of Surrey, along with a bevy of knights (totaling about a third of the English army), northward to assess the castle. The Scots immediately sent word to King John, who was camped with the main army inland near Haddington, requesting reinforcements. John sent most of the army to rescue Dunbar, but rather than saving the castle, they suffered a speedy and humiliating defeat. Though the Scots had an advantageous position on high ground, they misjudged the English army's actions. Mistakenly thinking they were retreating, the Scots charged downhill in a confused fashion, leaving the safety of the hill behind them. They encountered the English in formation and were routed immediately. In addition to the casualties, the disaster resulted in at least 100 lords, knights and soldiers taken prisoner, including John Comyn, who was taken with the others to England.[15]

---

[14] On the capture of Berwick, see John Parker Lawson, *Historical Tales of the Wars of Scotland, and of the Border Raids, Forays, and Conflicts* (Edinburgh: Fullarton, 1849), pp. 113-116.
[15] On the Battle of Dunbar, see Magnus Magnusson, *Scotland: The Story of a Nation* (New York: Grove Press,

With the Scottish army now virtually annihilated, Edward soon took the castles at Roxburgh, Edinburgh, Stirling, and Perth. Some, perhaps most famously Roxburgh, were surrendered with only the smallest attempt at a defense, while Edinburgh castle withstood for a week against Edward's siege machines. The English found Stirling castle completely abandoned, save for a caretaker who stayed back to leave the keys with the invading army. As these strongholds fell with ease into Edward's hand, the war was effectively over only a few months after it had begun. All that remained was for King John to surrender.

A statue commemorating Wallace at Edinburgh Castle today.

2000).

Following this quick succession of surrenders, John and some remaining lords fled to northeast Scotland, but it was soon clear to all that the Scottish monarch had no choice but to admit defeat and yield to Edward. On July 2, John officially begged forgiveness of Edward in a pleading letter. Edward accepted the surrender, but only after subjecting John to a humiliating ceremony on July 10, during which the deposed Scottish monarch had to renounce the treaty with France, apologize personally to Edward, and have the arms of Scotland formally stripped from his surcoat, earning him the nickname "Toom Tabard" ("empty coat"). John and his son Edward were transported to England, and John was imprisoned in the Tower of London until July 1299, when he was allowed to leave for France to be placed under the custody of Pope Boniface VIII.[16]

After that, the victorious Edward was bent on destroying any remaining Scottish identity or hints of Scottish independence. He had records related to the Scottish throne sent to London, and, as a spoil of war, he captured the sacred Stone of Scone from Scone Abbey in Perth. The stone had been used for centuries as the seat of coronation for Scottish monarchs, but after Edward had it transported to Westminster Abbey in London, it was fitted into a wooden chair and used for the coronation ceremonies of the English monarchs, a potent symbol of England's claim over Scotland.[17] Along with it, Edward also carted off the Scottish Crown Jewels and one of Scotland's holiest relics, the Black Rood of St. Margaret, which was believed to be a piece of the True Cross.

Edward's objective was nothing less than the destruction of Scotland and the total absorption of its people into his kingdom. To the latter end, he demanded oaths of fealty from Scots in acknowledgment of his overlordship. In late August 1296, nearly 1600 Scottish nobles and magnates made a personal oath to Edward by signing the Ragman's Roll, while any prominent Scot who failed to take this pledge was declared an outlaw and pursued by authorities. Among the thousands of names on the Roll was a minor landholder of Ayrshire named Alan Wallace, but even if that was William's father, Edward had no way of knowing that the son of this middling-rank crown tenant would, within only a year's time, cause him to lose control of Scotland.

Chapter 5: Wallace's Emergence

While Edward was well prepared for his 1296 invasion and the common army of Scots was nowhere near ready for war with England, he would be caught off guard in 1297 when Wallace and other leaders of the Scottish revolt used unconventional and unpredictable tactics. Indeed, Wallace sprang into the Scottish Wars of Independence in a dramatic fashion.

Despite Edward's crushing defeat of the country in 1296, armed resistance to English occupation of Scotland broke out by May 1297, with disturbances in both the northeast and

---

[16] G. P. Stell, "John [John de Balliol] (c.1248x50-1314)," *Oxford Dictionary of National Biography*.
[17] The Stone of Scone was returned to Scotland on St. Andrew's Day, November 30 1996, 700 years after it was stolen by King Edward. See David John Breeze and Graeme Munro, *The Stone of Destiny: Symbol of Nationhood*, (Edinburgh, 1997).

southwest parts of the country. As the flames of revolt spread across Scotland, Wallace entered the fray, and though hard facts about his initial war efforts are difficult to source, what is clear is that he emerged from obscurity in May 1297 by murdering the English sheriff of Lanark, William De Hesilrig. Heselrig was part of the English administration Edward had imposed on Scotland following his conquest the previous year, and at the head of this administration was John de Warenne, 6th Earl of Surrey, who had been Edward's chief lieutenant during the Battle of Dunbar. Assisting Warenne was Hugh of Cressingham, who served as treasurer.

With a trusted administration in place and confident in the finality of his conquest, Edward left England in 1296 to prepare for war with France, but unrest spread within months, with disturbances occurring throughout Scotland from the west highlands to Aberdeenshire and to Galloway in the southwest. In the north, Andrew Murray, Wallace's noted ally who was captured at the battle of Dunbar in 1296 but managed to escape imprisonment during the winter of 1296-1297, led a fierce resistance to English rule. Warenne and Cressingham mismanaged the mounting troubles, and the hostilities quickly spread.

Wallace's slaying of Heselrig in May marked an important turning point in the unrest, as what had previously been disjointed resistance turned into full-blown rebellion. As sheriff, Heselrig was a symbol of the repressive English authority, and at the time of his murder, he was in Lanark to hold an assize, a court session for the trial of civil or criminal cases. It would seem that Wallace chose his target and the occasion carefully, as the murder of an English official while he was exercising the king's legal authority over the Scots would have sent a powerful message to both the occupiers and the occupied.

Precisely what Wallace was doing in Lanark (in central Scotland) in May 1297 is unknown, but popular tradition claims he was there to seek personal revenge against Heselrig. The legend, stemming from Blind Harry's account of Wallace, holds that Heselrig had murdered Wallace's beloved Marion Braidfute, the heiress of Lamington, a village not far from Lanark. It is not clear whether Braidfute was Wallace's wife or mistress, but most historians treat the story of Wallace's hot-blooded, vengeful murder of Heselrig as myth and Marion Braidfute as part of this legend, since no evidence supports the personal vengeance claim.[18] It is far more likely that Wallace's brutal murder of Heselrig was intended to send a chilling message to the English that no one, not even officials, would be spared in the mounting rebellion. The English declared Wallace an outlaw, but many Scots were inspired by his actions and joined his campaign. Immediately after Lanark, Wallace's forces grew, spurred on perhaps by the rumor that Edward was looking to suppress midland Scotland in order to force the men of that region into his army to fight against France.[19]

---

[18] On Marion Braidfute as legend, see Fisher, *William Wallace*, pp. 37-38; and, *The Biographical Dictionary of Scottish Women,* eds. Elizabeth Ewan et. al. (Edinburgh: Edinburgh University Press, 2006).

[19] On this claim, see Andrew Fisher, "Wallace, Sir William (d. 1305)," *Oxford Dictionary of National Biography*, (Oxford: Oxford University Press, 2004).

Soon after Lanark, Wallace targeted another higher-ranking English official: William Ormsby, Edward's justiciar. Ormsby, the monarch's chief minister, was in Scone, 80 miles to the north of Lanark. Joined by the nobleman Sir William Douglar "le Hardi," another formidable fighter for the cause, Wallace aimed to capture Ormsby, but somehow the justiciar learned of the plot and fled Scone before his would-be captors arrived. Despite losing the main target, the raid was successful in that Wallace and Douglas captured the booty Ormsby left behind in his hurried state, further encouraging their fellow Scots to rally behind the rebellion.[20]

Following Scone, Wallace and Douglas parted ways, with the former heading toward the Selkirk (present-day Ettrick) Forest, where he headquartered his army. There Wallace waited while the English began to take a more active stance against the Scottish rebellion. In June 1297, the English, led by Henry Percy and Robert Clifford, crossed into Annandale from Cumberland and burnt Lochmaden on their way to Irvine. A Scottish army under the leadership of Douglas, Robert Wishart (the bishop of Glasgow), James Stewart (one of the former Guardians of Scotland), and a recent convert to the patriotic cause, Robert the Bruce, gathered to face the English threat. Not long after the English cavalry advanced against them, the Scots sought to negotiate terms of surrender, but the negotiations were unusually lengthy, a fact that has led some historians to argue that the negotiated surrender was merely a ruse to give Wallace more time to assemble an army.[21] Cressingham, Edward's treasurer, distrusted the Scots and raised an army to fight Wallace, but he was stopped by Percy and Clifford, who believed they had successfully pacified Scotland south of Lanark.

As it turned out, the English military leaders had underestimated their opponents. Following the capitulation at Irvine in July 1297, the Scots failed to surrender the hostages they had promised the English, and Stewart and Bruce rejoined the Scottish forces only a short time later. Wallace had since left the Forest of Selkirk to head north, where, according to Blind Harry, he burnt 100 English ships. Historian Andrew Fisher believes that was more likely the work of Andrew Murray[22], but either way, Wallace went on to push out the English from Fife and Perthshire. By August, he was laying siege to Dundee, and according to the chronicler Walter of Guisborough, Wallace had attained a large and diverse following: "the common folk of the land followed him as their leader and ruler; the retainers of the great lords adhered to him; and even though the lords themselves were present with the English king in body, at heart they were on the opposite side."[23]

It was at this moment, and with this widespread support, that Wallace began preparing for his

---

[20] On the Ormsby affair, see A.F. Murison, *William Wallace: Guardian of Scotland* (New York: Dover Publications, 2003, 1898), p. 76-77.
[21] On this, see *The Chronicle of Walter of Guisborough*, ed. H. Rothwell, (London: Butler & Tanner Ltd., 1957). Also G.W.S. Barrow, *Robert the Bruce: And the Community of the Realm of Scotland* (Edinburgh: Edinburgh University Press, 2005), p. 84.
[22] See Andrew Fisher, "Wallace, Sir William (d. 1305)," *Oxford Dictionary of National Biography*, (Oxford: Oxford University Press, 2004).
[23] See *The Chronicle of Walter of Guisborough*, ed. H. Rothwell, p. 299.

most famous battle: the battle of Stirling Bridge.

Chapter 6: The Battle of Stirling Bridge

Stirling Bridge today, with a monument to Wallace in the background.

The authority King Edward had reclaimed over Scotland the previous year was all but gone by the late summer of 1297. At the time, his treasurer, Cressingham, sent to his monarch the following assessment of the situation: "By far the greater part of your counties of the realm of Scotland are still unprovided with keepers...some have given up their bailiwicks, and others neither will nor dare return; and in some counties the Scots have established and placed bailiffs and ministers, so that no county is in proper order, excepting Berwick and Roxburgh, and this only lately."[24] Finally acknowledging that the Scottish rebellion was strong and growing, the English at last aimed to take firm action. Warenne, Edward's chief lieutenant who had succeeded at Dunbar in 1296, left Berwick and headed for Stirling with a sizeable army. Accompanied by Cressingham, they arrived near Stirling in early September.

Meanwhile, Wallace left the siege of the castle at Dundee to the town's inhabitants and also headed to Stirling, having joined forces with Andrew Murray, whose successful rebellion in the north of Scotland had severely weakened the English there. Together, the two headed what the

---

[24] *Documents Illustrative of the History of Scotland, Volume II*, ed. Rev. J. Stevenson (Edinburgh: H.M. General Register House, 1870), p. 207.

English called "a very large body of rogues," and in early September they took up position on the southward-looking slope of the Abbey Craig, about a mile north of a narrow wooden bridge stretching across the River Forth. This bridge, situated near Stirling Castle, was highly strategic, because the river was too deep and wide to cross below Stirling, and to the west lay Flanders Moss, marshland that was impossible to cross with an army. Furthermore, Stirling Bridge tied the north and south of Scotland together, so whoever controlled this site would hold a strategic advantage over the opponent.

A picture of the northern side across the Stirling Bridge where Wallace's army was located. Photo by Kim Traynor.

Wallace and Murray, even with their entire Scottish army in the field, were about to face a test of strength. The English army, with its heavy cavalry, outnumbered the Scots by a comfortable margin, a fact that might have caused Warenne to expect another easy victory like at Dunbar. He and Cressingham also had the advantage of experience on their side, since neither Wallace nor Murray could claim extensive military practice and neither had ever before commanded a large force. However, despite these clear advantages, Warenne did not seem bent on engaging in battle. In the days before the battle, he sent representatives to negotiate the surrender of the Scots, and when that failed, he sent two Dominican friars as envoys to speak with Wallace and Murray in order to procure from them terms for surrender. Much to Warenne's surprise, he received in response not a capitulation, but Wallace's well-known rebuff: "Go back and tell your people that we have not come here for peace: we are ready, rather, to fight to avenge ourselves and to free our country. Let them come up to us as soon as they like, and they will fund us prepared to prove the same in their beards."[25]

Hearing Wallace's slight, Warenne ordered an attack. Early on the morning of September 11, 1297, the English army, led by Cressingham, began to cross Stirling Bridge at a painstakingly slow pace, as the bridge was wide enough for only two horsemen to stand abreast. However, even after some 5,000 made it across, Warenne, who had overslept that morning and arrived late to the site, promptly recalled all of them. Warenne convened a Council of War, but he ignored the wise advice of a former Scottish knight, Richard Lundie, who had suggested crossing the river with his cavalry at a nearby ford where 60 horsemen could traverse together, in order to outflank the Scots. Cressingham preferred the bridge crossing, and Warenne deferred to his opinion.

As a result, within a few hours, the army again began a slow crossing of the bridge. Wallace and Murray observed the enemy's maneuvers from the Abbey Crag and waited until a certain number of the enemy had reached their side of the river. Once satisfied, they ordered their infantry down the slope along the narrow causeway to the bridge. The English cavalry, whose horses were unable to gain solid ground on the marshy terrain, floundered as the Scots seized the northern end of the bridge, thereby cutting off the advancing force from the rest of the army and from the hope of reinforcements. While the rest of the English army watched, the Scots annihilated or let drown some 5,000 infantry and 100 knights, including Cressingham, whose body was flayed and made into trophies. Tradition holds that Cressingham's skin was used to make Wallace's sword belt; the Lanercost Chronicle reported that Wallace had "a broad strip...taken from the head to the heel, to make therewith a baldrick for his sword."[26]

While Cressingham and the men on the other side of the bridge suffered their grisly fates, Warenne never crossed the bridge. As he witnessed the slaughter of his men from afar, he now had to worry about preventing the Scots from crossing the river in pursuit of what remained of the English army, so Warenne ordered the bridge's destruction and then promptly fled back to

---

[25] *The Chronicle of Walter of Guisborough*, ed. H. Rothwell, p. 300.
[26] Andrew Fisher discusses the battle of Stirling Bridge in *William Wallace*, pp. 110-159.

Berwick.

Naturally, the battle is best remembered for the way in which Blind Harry described it, even as his fantastical account is filled with inaccuracies:

> "On Saturday they [Murray and Wallace] rode on to the bridge, which was of good plain board, well made and jointed, having placed watches to see that none passed from the army. Taking a wright, the most able workman there, he [Wallace] ordered him to saw the plank in two at the mid streit [middle stretch], so that no-one might walk over it. He then nailed it up quickly with hinges, and dirtied it with clay, to cause it to appear that nothing had been done. The other end he so arranged that it should lie on three wooden rollers, which were so placed, that when one was out the rest would fall down. The wright, himself, he ordered to sit there underneath, in a cradle, bound on a beam, to loose the pin when Wallace let him know by blowing a horn when the time was come. No one in all the army should be allowed to blow but he himself.
>
> The day of the great battle approached; for power, the English would not fail; they were ever six to one against Wallace. Fifty thousand made for the place of battle, the remainder abiding at the Castle; both field and Castle they thought to conquer at their will. The worthy Scots upon the other side of the river, took the plain field on foot.
>
> Hugh Cressingham leads on the vanguard with twenty thousand likely men to see. Thirty thousand the Earl of Warren had, but he did then as wisdom did direct, all the first army being sent over before him. Some Scottish men, who well knew this manner of attack, bade Wallace sound, saying there were now enough. He hastened not, however, but steadily observed the advance until he saw Warren's force thickly crowd the bridge. Then from Jop he took the horn and blew loudly, and warned John the Wright, who thereupon struck out the roller with skill; when the pin was out, the rest of it fell down. Now arose an hideous outcry among the people, both horses and men, falling into the water. (...)
>
> On foot, and bearing a great sharp spear, Wallace went amongst the thickest of the press. he aimed a stroke at Cressingham in his corslet, which was brightly polished. The sharp head of the spear pierced right through the plates and through his body, stabbing him beyond rescue; thus was that chieftain struck down to death. With the stroke Wallace bore down both man and horse.
>
> The English army although ready for battle, lost heart when their chieftain was slain, and many openly began to flee. Yet worthy men abode in the place until ten thousand were slain. Then the remainder fled, not able to abide longer, seeking

succour in many directions, some east, some west, and some fled to the north. Seven thousand full at once floated in the Forth, plunged into the deep and drowned without mercy; none were left alive of all that fell army."

  Regardless of the subsequent embellishments, Wallace and Murray's achievement at Stirling Bridge was nothing less than remarkable. Despite their inferior numbers, and an army composed of a ragtag host of peasants, farmers and burgesses, the two leaders exploited the terrain and outwitted and outmaneuvered the far more experienced Warenne and his heavy cavalry. The effects of this resounding victory were felt immediately too. Dundee and Stirling castles surrendered, while the towns Edinburgh and Berwick also fell to the Scots (though their castles remained in English hands). When the towns of Haddington and Roxburgh were burnt, English hold over Scotland had been all but eliminated.

  While the victory at Stirling Bridge decisively swung the war's momentum behind the Scots, it came at a cost. Andrew Murray was grievously injured during the battle and died in early November. Despite his injuries, over the two months between Stirling Bridge and his death, Murray and Wallace worked together as leaders not only of the Scottish army but of the country as a whole. In October, the two sent missives to the mayors and communes of Hamburg and Lübeck in an attempt to restore trading relations with Germany, and in early November, Wallace followed up this attempt at diplomacy by securing the election of William Lamberton, who turned out to be staunchly anti-English, as the bishop of St. Andrews. Around that time, Murray passed away from the wounds he had sustained at Stirling Bridge, leaving the burden of defending Scotland solely on Wallace's shoulders. For the next year, Wallace would hold the highest rank of power and authority in Scotland.

A stained glass depiction of Wallace in Stirling

Chapter 7: Chief of Scotland

A William Wallace statue located in Aberdeen

With momentum on his side, Wallace went on the offensive against England, and by the end of October 1297, he had invaded English territory by marching his growing army into Northumberland and taking its inhabitants by surprise. From Northumberland, Wallace led his men across the northwest of England, arriving as far as Cockermouth. While it sounds particularly bold, Wallace was at least partly forced to march into England because Scotland was stricken by famine and his army, which had grown markedly in size, needed more resources.

It was during this period that Wallace earned the reputation among the English as a ruthless and violent brute. Without siege machines, the Scottish army could not take any English cities of consequence, so they resorted to raiding and pillaging less-protected towns. According to Walter of Guisborough, "the services of God totally ceased in all the monasteries and churches between Newcastle and Carlisle, for all the canons, monks and priests fled before the face of the Scots, as did nearly all the people."[27] The reputation for ferocity and barbarity that Wallace gained at this

---

[27] *The Chronicle of Walter of Guisborough*, ed. H. Rothwell, p. 304.

time remained with him for centuries after his death, even though, as Andrew Fisher claims, the cruel acts he ordered were "like those ordered by Edward I at Berwick," and were "of a kind often repeated by both sides."[28] By late November, after a failed attempt to raid the bishopric of Durham, the severe weather forced the end of the invasion of England. Wallace and his troops returned north.

    Back in Scotland, Wallace set about preparing for the inevitable return of the English army and securing his role as the country's military leader. To do that, he had to contend with quite a few thorny issues. Many Scottish nobles resented Wallace's quick rise to power, and according to some contemporaries, Wallace didn't hesitate to use harsh measures against his detractors at home. Stories of imprisonment and hangings made the rounds in both Scotland and England, confirming in the eyes of the English Wallace's status as a violent brigand.[29] In fact, it was a shared sentiment that Wallace should be defeated that brought the English people together in support of their monarch's renewed campaign in Scotland. In the winter of 1297-1298, Edward had been in Flanders overseeing his campaign against France, and he did not return to England until March 1298 after a truce was negotiated with the French. Almost immediately, he set about preparing for war with the Scots and even transferred the seat of government north to York in order to be closer to his target. In April, he convened a war council in York to plan a campaign, but the Scottish magnates ordered to attend ignored his directive. In retaliation, Edward announced the forfeiture of their lands.

    On June 25, the king's army assembled at Roxburgh, and Edward joined them by early July. Edward headed a strong force composed of roughly 2,000-3,000 horsemen and about 14,000 infantry, many of whom were Welsh, but as he led the army north and advanced into Scotland through Lauderdale, he found the land devastated and empty of inhabitants, which deprived him of the opportunity to gain intelligence about the Scottish army's whereabouts.

    While Edward's preparations for war are well known, Wallace's own actions during this time are far less understood. In fact, it is impossible to place him between his return to Scotland in November 1297, following the raid of northern England, and March 1298, when documents show his presence at Porphichen in Linlithgowshire on March 29th. However, these documents also reveal that by March 1298, Wallace had two new titles: knight and guardian of the kingdom, both in addition to his already established role as leader of the army. He was the first Scot to be the sole holder of the second title, guardian of the kingdom. The dates he received these titles are unknown, but it's safe to assume the military prowess he exhibited throughout 1297 was the reason they were bestowed on him. Of course, to Edward, Wallace's titles meant nothing.

    By the summer of 1298, Edward's sole aim was to locate and subsequently annihilate Sir William and his motley army, but Wallace was not eager to engage in battle with the English and

---

[28] Andrew Fisher, "Wallace, Sir William (d. 1305)," *Oxford Dictionary of National Biography*.
[29] *Calendar of documents relating to Scotland*, ed. J. Bain, vol. 2, no. 1689.

thus engaged in a shrewd strategy of withdrawal, heading ever farther north and leaving nothing but scorched earth behind him. Edward took the bait and continued advancing deeper into Scotland, overstretching his lines of communication and supplies just as Wallace had hoped. Unable to locate the enemy or live off the land, his army was soon starving and in disarray. On July 19, when the army was at Temple Liston, a large supply of wine reached them, and Edward promptly distributed it. The Welsh soldiers became drunk and ended up rioting, killing several priests. Edward unleashed his cavalry on them, and 80 Welsh soldiers were killed. Many others threatened to change sides before the outbreak was finally quelled. Following this clash, Edward decided to retire to Edinburgh.[30] Wallace's strategy was working, and he was yet again outwitting King Edward.

Chapter 8: The Battle of Falkirk

Edward was on the verge of retreat when fortune finally smiled on him on July 21; two earls had a messenger convey intelligence to the king that Wallace and his men were stationed at Falkirk, less than 20 miles away. The messenger also informed Edward of Wallace's intention to attack the retreating English army by night. Edward acted at once and immediately directed his army toward Falkirk. That night they camped near the Scottish forces, and the king ordered his men to sleep with their horses beside them in case the Scots attacked. Chaos soon ensued when Edward himself was injured by his horse and the soldiers panicked, and it was only by mounting his horse to display his strength that the king was able to calm his men. At sunrise the next morning, he led his army toward Falkirk.

Edward came upon Wallace in a strongly entrenched position, protected by a morass which was hidden from the English. Though Wallace had attempted to avoid battle, he at least found himself in a strong position when Edward surprised him with his men arranged to fight. When the English spotted them, the Scots were divided into four schiltroms, the core Scottish battle strategy. A schiltrom was a formation of as many as 2,000 men brandishing 12 foot-long spears and gathered in either huge circles or rectangles to look something like a lethal hedgehog. The ranks of the schiltrom were to be packed tightly so as to be nearly impenetrable. With this formation, the Scottish infantry could face off against mounted cavalrymen, England's strongest weapon. Between the schiltroms, Wallace had stationed his archers, and behind everyone stood the modest-sized Scottish cavalry, under the command of John Comyn.

Despite having a clear advantage, as well as the benefit of the element of surprise, Edward preferred not to engage immediately and instructed his army to rest. However, several men, including the earls of Norfolk, Hereford, and Lincoln, refused to follow his order and led a unit forward toward the Scots. They were blocked from advancing further by the morass and had to shift westward, splitting into two wings. Once past the marshland, the English vanguard clashed with the schiltroms, who held their positions and managed to inflict heavy damage on the

---

[30] On this incident, see Andrew Fisher, "Wallace, Sir William (d. 1305)," *Oxford Dictionary of National Biography*.

English cavalry. In response, Edward called up his archers to weaken the Scottish ranks.

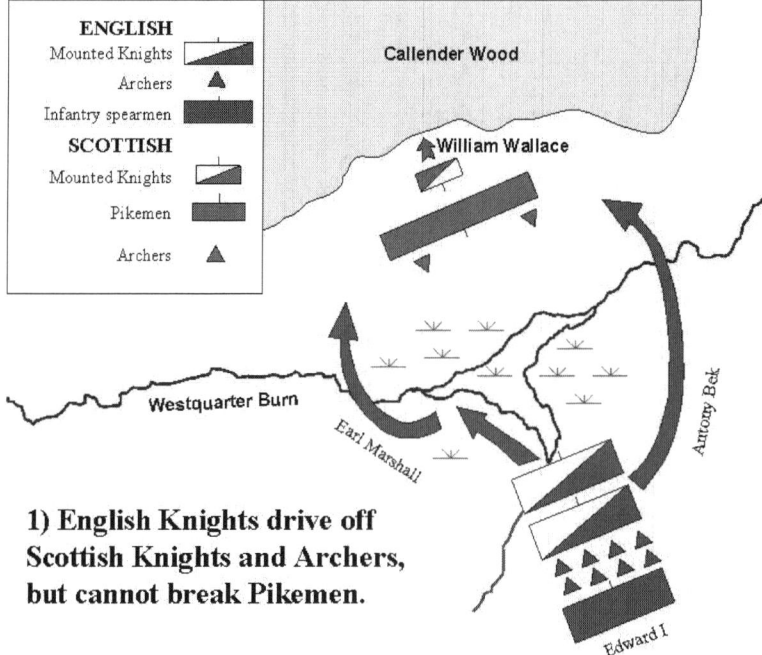

Map of the early action at Falkirk made by Mike Young

When Edward called up the archers, the Scottish cavalry fled, leaving the schiltroms and the Scottish archers with no rear support, but even with a barrage of arrows falling on them, the schiltroms managed to keep their discipline. While they were suffering heavy losses, they also killed more than 100 English horsemen, but Wallace was severely weakened without his cavalry, which became even more evident once Edward withdrew his cavalry and advanced his longbowmen and crossbowmen. The Scottish infantry was massacred by both the hail of arrows and a series of renewed cavalry assaults.[31]

---

[31] On this battle, see Andrew Fisher, *William Wallace*, pp. 138-144.

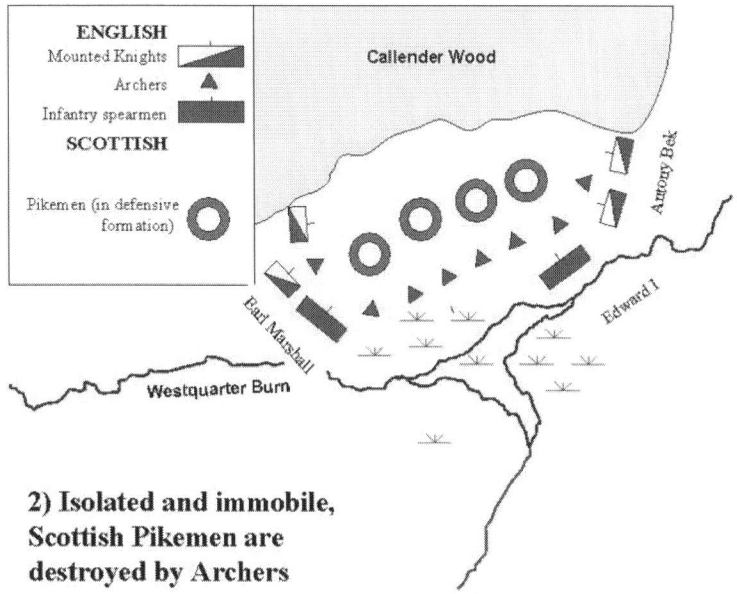

2) Isolated and immobile, Scottish Pikemen are destroyed by Archers

Map by Mike Young

Wallace left the field with a small force before the battle was over, but while the English charged him with cowardice, he was apparently working to ensure the escape of Scottish survivors, many of whom fled into the nearby woods. Wallace headed toward Stirling and burnt the town and the castle once he arrived. Though Edward had won at Falkirk, his army was too depleted to carry on the campaign or to pursue Wallace, so he began to withdraw his troops and was back in Carlisle by September 9.

With that, Edward's fight for Scotland was temporarily suspended, and the same could be said for Wallace. Some time between the battle of Falkirk and the following December, Wallace resigned the guardianship, which was taken over by Robert the Bruce and John Comyn. He traveled to the European continent, where he presented Scotland's case for freedom to various courts. Evidence from the time suggests that despite his failure at Falkirk, many Scots still supported Wallace and considered his efforts in Europe to be for the good of the kingdom.[32]

As it turned out, diplomacy proved to be nearly as dangerous as warfare. It is difficult to know

---

[32] See G.W. S. Barrow, *Robert the Bruce*, p. 107.

for certain where Wallace went first, and some believe he visited Norway before arriving in France in early November 1299 to lobby for King Philip IV's support. What is clear though is that rather than listening to Wallace's case, Philip had him arrested and offered to hand him over to the English. The cause of the king's sudden loyalty to the English, his former enemies, was Edward's marriage to his sister Margaret only two months earlier. However, when Edward learned that Wallace was in French captivity, he responded with a surprising lack of interest and urgency. He merely thanked Philip and requested that he keep Wallace in France until further notice.

There is no clear explanation for Edward's apparent apathy, and speculation suggests that the English king was not bent on Wallace's destruction. Perhaps he considered the Scot too removed and far from the Scottish cause and thus no longer a real threat, but whatever Edward's thinking, he made absolutely no attempt to have Wallace brought to England for justice. After a year of watching over Wallace, Philip grew fond of him and released him to carry on his diplomatic campaigns elsewhere.

It is possible, though not provable, that Wallace headed to Rome from France. In the spring of 1301, a Scottish delegation was in Rome to refute Edward's claim to Scotland, a mission Wallace would likely have been eager to join. Beyond this possibility, nothing else is known about his time on the continent or the other courts he may have visited. Indeed, Wallace does not appear in any records again until 1303, when he was back on the battlefields of Scotland fighting the English.

Chapter 9: Fighting Again

The precise date of Wallace's return to Scotland is unknown, but during his time in France, the political dynamics at home were evolving. William Lamberton, the Bishop of St. Andrews, was selected to serve as the third Guardian in order to help keep the peace between Bruce and Comyn, who were frequently as odds with each other. The Scottish army also recaptured Stirling Castle.

In May 1300, Edward launched yet another campaign in Scotland to bring the country under his permanent control. He focused in particular on securing the castles, and after invading Galloway, he laid siege to Caerlaverock castle near the southern coast south of Dumfries. Siege engines were transported from Lochmaben and surrounding castles in order to force out the 60 Scots trying to defend the stronghold against the much larger English army, and once Edward finally broke through the defenses, he hanged several of the Scottish fighters from the castle's battlements. However, aside from a few other minor skirmishes, the English campaign of 1300 achieved little else of significance beside rebuke from outsiders; that August, the papacy sent a letter imploring Edward to withdraw from Scotland.

Over the spring and summer of the next four years, 1301-1304, Edward continued to lead campaigns north into Scotland with the view of bringing the territory definitively under his control, and in 1302, his authority increased when Robert the Bruce submitted to him. Later the same year, even the papacy softened its stance on his place in Scottish affairs, as Pope Boniface VIII wrote to the Scottish bishops encouraging them to reconcile with Edward. As his hold over Scotland grew more secure, Edward resurrected old practices, such as demanding that the Scottish nobles pay homage to him. He also re-established an English administration, including English sheriffs in all strategic localities, to run several aspects of Scotland's political and legal systems.

Portrait of Pope Boniface VIII

During Edward's operations in 1303, however, he experienced difficulties early on due to sustained opposition posed by Wallace, who repeatedly hindered both divisions of the English army from advancing. The king and his men eventually made his way across most of Scotland before settling for the winter near Dunfermline, and by early 1304, the tides turned in Edward's favor. On February 9, John Comyn submitted to him, followed by all of the leading and influential Scots except Wallace and a few others. Perhaps one of the reasons Wallace didn't submit is because it wasn't a palatable option; had Wallace chosen to submit to Edward, he would not have enjoyed the same lenient terms granted to both Bruce and Comyn because Edward all but excluded him from this option: "as for Sir William Wallace, it is agreed that he may render himself up to the will and mercy of our sovereign lord the king, if it shall seem good to him."[33] In other words, if Wallace surrendered, no clemency was guaranteed.

According to an English chronicle, Wallace had sought through friends to arrange an occasion to submit to Edward in early 1304, but the proposal so infuriated the English king that he offered a reward to any man who killed Wallace instead. Edward had Wallace officially outlawed at a parliament held at St. Andrews in March 1304, along with the garrison of Stirling, which also failed to give in to the king. By May 1304, when almost all of the Scottish opposition had been eliminated, Edward set his sights on taking the castle at Stirling Bridge, no doubt considering the symbolic significance of capturing the stronghold of a site where his men suffered a humiliating defeat six years earlier. For three months, he used every siege machine in his arsenal to attack Stirling castle, but to no avail. Finally, he had a massive trebuchet built, called the "Warwolf," which was capable of hurling boulders at the castle's walls. After holding out for more than three months, the defenders surrendered within a day of the first use of the Warwolf.[34]

With nearly all of the powerful Scots in his back pocket and Stirling castle now in his possession, Edward intensified his efforts to capture the elusive Wallace. In March 1304, he had sent a large force, which included Robert the Bruce, to fight against the Scottish hero, but it failed to capture him. During a skirmish in September 1304, Wallace again managed to escape the English army, but only after inflicting considerable casualties on the army. In response, Edward increased the stakes with bribery and coercion by promising several Scots who had submitted to him, including Comyn, to commute their sentences of exile in return for Wallace's capture.

Despite the intense pressure on Wallace, it would take Edward nearly another full year to find and detain him. How he lived at large until then is unknown, as no documents make reference to his movements or actions, but on August 3, 1305, Edward finally got his wish when Wallace was taken by one of his fellow Scots, John Menteith, the keeper of Dumbarton Castle. Menteith was rewarded with land for his compliance.

Chapter 10: Wallace's End

"Schyre Jhon of Menteith in tha days

Tuk in Glasgow William Walays;

And sent hym until Ingland sune,

There was he quartayrd and undone." – Metrical Chronicle, 1418

---

[33] Cited in Andrew Fisher, "Wallace, Sir William (d. 1305)," *Oxford Dictionary of National Biography*.
[34] For a discussion of Edward's use of the Warwolf, see Michael Prestwich, *Edward I* (Berkeley: University of California Press, 1988), p. 502.

Edward refused to meet with Wallace following his arrest and had him transported to London on August 22. In the early morning of the next day, Wallace arrived and was taken on horseback in a procession of judicial and legal authorities to Westminster Hall. There was frenzied excitement on the streets as many Londoners came out to catch a glimpse of the notorious Scottish warrior.

Inside the hall, Wallace was accompanied onto a scaffold, where officials placed a laurel crown on his head in an apparent attempt to humiliate him by deeming him merely a king of outlaws, as it was the only crown they believed he merited. The justice presiding over the "trial" presented the indictment, accusing Wallace of treason and engaging in war crimes by "sparing neither age nor sex, monk nor nun." While admitting to the other allegations, Wallace denied the charge of treason, replying, "I could not be a traitor to Edward, for I was never his subject." No examination of evidence took place, nor was any testimony of witness heard; Wallace was not permitted to defend himself because his legal status was that of an outlawed thief.

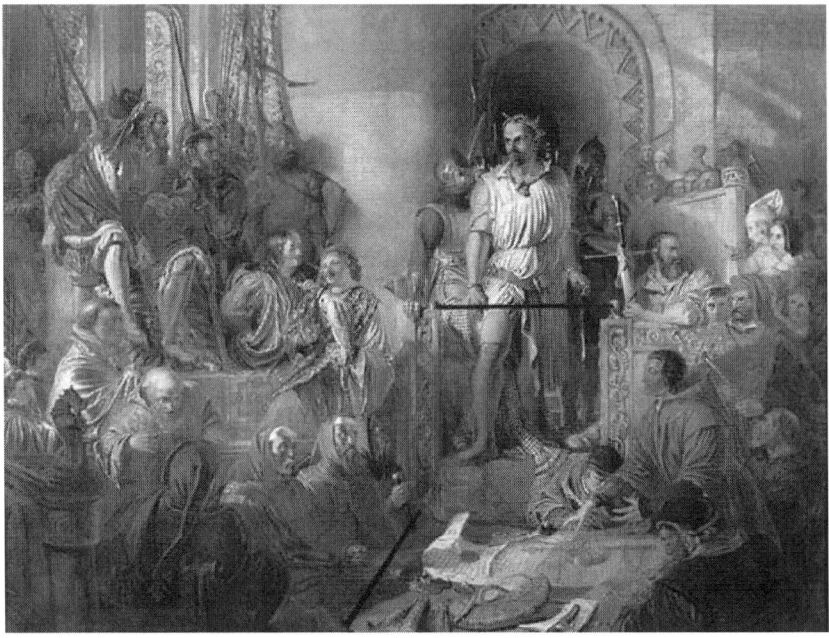

Daniel Maclise's painting, *The Trial of William Wallace at Westminster*

Obviously, the proceedings were a mere formality, and the judgment was given on the same day. William Wallace was found guilty of treason against the English king for taking up arms against him in Scotland and for making an alliance with France, and he received the standard sentence for treason. He was to be drawn to the gallows on a hurdle by horses through the streets of London, where he would be hanged for the crimes of murder and robbery. As a desecrator of churches, he was to be cut down from the gallows while not quite dead in order that his internal organs and genitals be removed and burned. Finally, as an outlaw, his head was cut off and placed on London Bridge, while the remainder of his body was to be cut into quarters to be displayed in Newcastle, Berwick, Stirling, and Perth. As historian John Reuben Davies put it, "Wallace's execution is a classic scene from one of history's great tragedies: the death of a national hero, a bloodthirsty judicial killing, the demonstrative and exemplary justice of an English king."[35] A plaque now documents the spot near where he was executed on August 23, 1305.

---

[35] Andrew Fisher explains this sentence in, "Wallace, Sir William (d. 1305)," *Oxford Dictionary of National Biography*. Also see, John Reuben Davies, "The Execution of William Wallace: Saint Bartholomew's Eve, Monday 23 August 1305," *The Breaking of Britain: Cross Border Society and Scottish Independence, 1216-1314,* August 2013, http://www.breakingofbritain.ac.uk/blogs/feature-of-the-month/august-2013/.

Picture of the plaque located at St. Bartholomew's Hospital in London, taken by Steve F-E-Cameron

In the decades following his death, Wallace's legacy fell under the shadow of the rising Bruce dynasty. Robert the Bruce was crowned King of Scots on March 25, 1306, and the house of Bruce held the throne until 1371, when it passed to the Stewart family, whose dynasty lasted until 1707. Wallace, who throughout his life had raised the banner in the name of the Scottish king John Balliol, was not a celebrated figure in Scotland during the Bruce years.

It was Blind Harry, 170 years later, who rescued Wallace from potential obscurity with his heavily embellished epic poem celebrating the great warrior's achievements. Had it not been for Blind Harry's account, Wallace might not have been remembered so prominently as a leading protagonist in the Scottish Wars of Independence. Paradoxically, however, while Harry salvaged the memory of Wallace, he also obscured it with his dressed up version of the Scot's life. It has become the task of historians of the 20th and 21st centuries to put Wallace back into perspective and to attempt to determine the real details of his life as best as possible with the scant evidence available.

If anything, the efforts to piece together Wallace's biography reveal how unnecessary it was to exaggerate his life's narrative. Even based on the little that is known, it's evident that Wallace was a unique figure in history. In a socially rigid society, he rose from modest beginnings to become the leader of Scotland, and though he lacked formal or extensive training in warfare, he fought more successfully than perhaps anyone else against one of the best military kings in history. His life story was already the stuff of legend, with no need for extra gilding.

Bibliography

Barrow, G. W. S. (1989), Kingship and Unity: Scotland 1000–1306, The New History of Scotland 2 (2nd ed.), Edinburgh: Edinburgh University Press, ISBN 0-7486-0104-X, 4th edition (2005) ISBN 0748620222

Barrow, G. W. S. (1976), Robert Bruce and the Community of the Realm of Scotland (2nd ed.), Edinburgh: Edinburgh University Press, ISBN 0-85224-307-3

Brown, Chris (2005), William Wallace. The True Story of Braveheart, Stroud: Tempus Publishing Ltd, ISBN 0-7524-3432-2

Brown, Michael (2004), The Wars of Scotland 1214–1371, The New Edinburgh History of Scotland 4, Edinburgh: Edinburgh University Press, ISBN 0-7486-1238-6

Cowan, Edward J., ed. (2007), The Wallace Book, Edinburgh: John Donald, ISBN 978-0-85976-652-4

Cowan, Edward J. (2007), "William Wallace: 'The Choice of the Estates'", in Cowan, Edward J., The Wallace Book, Edinburgh: John Donald, pp. 9–25, ISBN 978-0-85976-652-4

Duncan, A. A. M. (2007), "William, Son of Alan Wallace: The Documents", in Cowan, Edward J., The Wallace Book, Edinburgh: John Donald, pp. 42–63, ISBN 978-0-85976-652-4

Fisher, Andrew (2002), William Wallace (2nd ed.), Edinburgh: Birlinn, ISBN 1-84158-593-9

Morton, Graeme. William Wallace. London: Sutton, 2004. ISBN 0-7509-3523-5.

Reese, Peter. William Wallace: A Biography. Edinburgh: Canongate, 1998. ISBN 0-86241-607-8.

Stead, Michael J., and Alan Young. In the Footsteps of William Wallace. London: Sutton, 2002.

Traquair, Peter (1998), Freedom's Sword, University of Virginia: Roberts Rinehart Publishers, ISBN 1570982473

Printed in Great Britain
by Amazon.co.uk, Ltd.,
Marston Gate.